Season of New Beginnings

Praying Through Lent with

Saint Augustine of Hippo
Dorothy Day
Vincent van Gogh
Saint Teresa of Avila
John Henry Newman
Flannery O'Connor

●

MITCH FINLEY

Resurrection Press
Mineola • New York

Other books by Mitch Finley:

Building Christian Families (with Kathy Finley; Thomas More Publications)

Catholic Spiritual Classics (Sheed & Ward)

Your Family in Focus: Appreciating What You Have, Making It Even Better (Ave Maria Press)

Everybody Has a Guardian Angel ... And Other Lasting Lessons I Learned in Catholic Schools (Crossroad Publishing Co.)

Heavenly Helpers: St. Anthony and St. Jude (Crossroad Publishing Co.)

Catholic Is Wonderful (Resurrection Press)

Whispers of Love: Encounters with Deceased Relatives and Friends (Crossroad Publishing Co.)

Season of Promises (Resurrection Press)

First published in February, 1996 by Resurrection Press, Ltd.
P.O. Box 248
Williston Park, NY 11596

Second printing – January, 1997

ISBN 1-878718-32-0

Cover design by John Murello

Printed in the United States of America.

This small book is for friends with whom my spouse,
Kathy, and I have shared good years and many:
years of growing from young marrieds
to "mature" couples, supporting one another
in the wild and sacred adventures of marriage
and parenthood all the while;
years during which we shared
tears of sorrow and tears of joy and laughter —
more of the latter than of the former.

Others have joined our small faith community
along the way, some have come and gone,
and we value their friendship immeasurably.

But this one is for all the "old-timers"
who still hang in there: Garrick and Lela Dung,
Hans and Mallene Herzog, Tony Lehmann, S.J.,
Steve and Beth Shafer, Jerry and Judie Van Pevenage,
George and Rita Waldref.

You guys are a holy hoot.
Thanks be to God.

Introduction

L ENT. It's a deceptively simple sounding, single-syllable word, a word neither soft nor hard, a word without a question mark that, all the same, carries a question. Here, Lent murmurs, its voice quiet but insistent, here is the question. Listen. Listen: Which side are you on? Are you on the side of Divine Foolishness or on the side of Never Take Any Chances? Do you side with those who seek a new heart and a new world, or do you side with those who cherish the status quo? Which side are you on?

Lent has forty days, a month and a week and a few more days. Lent is a season not of nature — not of Spring, Summer, Fall, Winter — but a season of the spirit. Lent is a season to become less self-centered, less narrow-minded; more other-centered, more broad-minded. It's a season to grow less cold-hearted, more warm-hearted. Lent is a season of new beginnings.

Lent hits us right between the eyes with ashes on Ash Wednesday. Then day after day, for forty days, it whispers in our heart. Lent whispers: "Remember that you are dust and to dust you shall return." It whispers, "Repent and believe in the gospel." It whispers, "Do grow up, oh small of heart, small of spirit." It whispers, "God loves you with an infinite, unconditional love, a love so high you can't get over it, so wide you can't get around it, so low you can't get under it...."

Lent whispers and whispers, and so...we need some quiet times if we want to hear what it says. We need five or ten

5

minutes in each of Lent's forty days when we do nothing but attend to what Lent may whisper in our heart. That's the purpose of the little book you hold in your hands. Think of it as a spiritual compass, something to give you some direction for a few minutes in each of Lent's forty days. Or, if you prefer, think of this small book as a literary sparkplug, something to keep the spirit of Lent alive for you one day at a time.

Each day's mini-meditation begins with a brief quotation from the writings of a spiritual guide. In rotation you will read the thoughtful words of Saint Augustine of Hippo (5th century), Saint Teresa of Avila (16th century), Cardinal John Henry Newman (19th century), Vincent van Gogh (19th century), Dorothy Day (20th century), and Flannery O'Connor (20th century). Following their words you will find a short reflection designed to put a "Lenten spin" on the words you just read, a perspective rooted in the realities of our own time and place and the season of Lent. Then, the capper, a one-line prayer. Say the prayer and let it sink in.

Read on, pilgrim. Steep yourself in the truth of Lent which is the truth of the living Christ, who in the Gospel of Mark begins his public ministry with words to echo in our ears for each one of Lent's forty days. Listen: "The time is fulfilled, and the kingdom of God has come near; repent, and believe in the good news" (1:15).

Ash Wednesday — First Day of Lent

*Late have I loved you, O Beauty, so ancient and so new,
late have I loved you! And behold, you were within me and I
was outside, and there I sought for you, and in my deformity
I rushed headlong into the well-formed things that you have
made. You were with me, and I was not with you.*

— SAINT AUGUSTINE OF HIPPO, *Confessions*

ISN'T THAT JUST THE WAY? God is with us, but we are not
with God. You want a reason for Lent? This is the reason for
Lent. Ashes smeared in a cross on the forehead, right between
the eyes, and they remind us that God is with us but we are
not with God, not nearly as close as we could be, at least. All
the same, we are not without hope. That's the reason for Lent.
We are not without hope, not by a long shot.

Saint Augustine, writing the first book ever written in the
first person, one thousand five hundred years ago, sounds as
contemporary as today's newspaper. Late have we loved our
God. But better late than never, better late than never. You
bet your bottom dollar. Lent hits us right between the eyes,
brings us up short, stops us in our tracks. Says: Better late
than never, and there's no time like the present.

So — the question comes flying through the air, hits us right
between the eyes — what are you doing for Lent? What are
you doing for Lent? Hm. Maybe going to pay closer attention this year to what *God* is doing for Lent? Never thought
of it that way before. What is God doing for Lent? What is
the Lord, the Holy of Holies, the Ruler of the Universe doing
for Lent?

Whoa. Going to have to keep our eyes open for that one,

alright. Could be the Lord of Lent holds surprises in store. Could be. You never know. We are not without hope, not by a long shot.

Loving God, Father of Mercies, Lord of Lent,
help me to pay close attention to what
you are doing for Lent this year. Amen.

✻   **Thursday — Second Day of Lent**   ✻

In the front room Mrs. Barrett was on her knees saying her prayers. She turned to tell me that Kathryn and the children had all gone to the store and went on with her praying. And I felt a warm burst of love towards Mrs. Barrett that I have never forgotten, a feeling of gratitude and happiness that still warms my heart when I remember her. She had God, and there was beauty and joy in her life.

— Dorothy Day, *Meditations*

CAN A PERSON "have God"? So it would seem. Astonishing as it seems. But having God is a consequence of God having us. Our loving God holds us at all times and in all places and so...we "have God."

Someone asked the great theologian Karl Rahner to summarize all his vast, complex theological writings in one sentence. So he did. He tapped his forehead with his finger and thought about it. He said, "God dwells in you." That's it. "God dwells in you," therefore you "have God." It's enough to make you fall over from sheer delight. Fall right over from sheer delight. If you think about it. Which, of course, we ordinarily do not.

Think of Lent as a time to put some extra effort into thinking about it. God dwells in you. Think about it, let it sink in. Fall right over from sheer delight. Sure, Lent is a time to fast and abstain, a penitential season, weeks to focus on conversion and repentance. But grim it need not be. We are grim enough most of the time. Maybe during Lent we need to work on being not so grim, more open to delight. Everyday delight.

Dorothy Day, co-founder of the Catholic Worker movement, thought about it, and she remembered that when she was a girl she had a neighbor who said her prayers on her knees in her front room. Mrs. Bennett "had God" and so "there was beauty and joy in her life." We, too, "have God," so there can be beauty and joy in our life, as well. Think of Lent as a time to let more beauty and joy into your life. Think of Lent as such a time. It's OK to smile during Lent.

God our loving Father, help me to be more aware
of your presence in me and in my life, and help me
to let more beauty and joy into my life. Amen.

✳   ## Friday — Third Day of Lent   ✳

Oh, that there were such an heart in us, to put aside this
visible world, to desire to look at it as a mere screen be-
tween us and God, and to think of Him who has entered in
beyond the veil, and who is watching us, trying us, yes, and
blessing, and influencing, and encouraging us towards good,
day by day! Yet, alas, how do we suffer the mere varying
circumstances of every day to sway us!

— JOHN HENRY NEWMAN, *Parochial and Plain Sermons*

T HE VISIBLE WORLD "a mere screen between us and God"?
Writing in 19th-century England, friend John Henry (nobody called him Jack) seems to attribute less value to "the visible world" than we do today. We find in creation more than "a mere screen between us and God." We find our natural environment, we find the place where we are meant to work out

our salvation. God showed great love by giving us the earth and all it contains.

And yet. And yet. John Henry had a point there. He had a point that rings true for us, even for us. "The visible world" is transparent, and if we look through it we will see God. "We are living in a transparent world," said Thomas Merton, "and God shines through in every moment." Our trouble is that we do not see, so much of the time we do not see. We see only what's on the surface. We "suffer the mere circumstances of every day to sway us." Do we ever. Lord knows.

Lent is a time for looking. So look. Rub the sleep out of your eyes and look through the veil to the other side. Break on through to the other side. See God shining through in every person, every tree, every daily happening, every forlorn sparrow perched on a telephone wire, each and every moment. See God shining through, "blessing, and influencing, and encouraging us towards good, day by day!"

Lord Jesus, help me to love this visible world as you did by coming into it and becoming one of us, and help me to see the Father's love shining through its every aspect. Amen.

Saturday — Fourth Day of Lent

Because we have heard and because faith tells us so, we know we have souls. But we seldom consider the precious things that can be found in this soul, or who dwells within it, or its high value. Consequently, little effort is made to preserve its beauty. All our attention is taken up with the plainness of the diamond's setting or the outer wall of the castle; that is, with these bodies of ours.

— Saint Teresa of Avila, *The Interior Castle*

W E DO NOT so much "have" a soul as we "are" a soul. Professional ponderers of things spiritual tell us that we are "embodied spirits." We are as much bodies as we are souls. Our bodily actions are also spiritual actions, and when we behave in explicitly spiritual ways we behave in bodily ways, too. Physical matters are spiritual matters, and spiritual matters are physical matters. Healthy eating habits and getting enough exercise are spiritual issues, and regular time for prayer, meditation, worship, and so forth, are physiological issues.

Can't separate the soul from the body and vice-versa. Not as long as body and soul are together. Lent is a crackerjack time to focus on body-soul unity. What are the spiritual implications of your eating habits? Exercise habits or lack thereof? Such questions are important because we have as much of a tendency to disregard our bodies as to disregard our souls. It's so easy to swing to one or the other. We may focus on "spiritual" concerns and ignore our habit of eating way too many Double Whammy Burgers with Giant Fries. Or we may scrupulously avoid fatty foods, keep our diet low in cholesterol, eat plenty of fresh vegetables and whole grain breads, and so forth, and starve ourselves spiritually.

What does it mean to nourish oneself spiritually? Prayer? Sure. Make a retreat? Natch. Fast and abstinence during Lent? Of course. But it also may include making time to relax and listen to good music or take a walk. If you're married it can mean taking the trouble to put some new life into making love with your spouse. If you have children it can mean taking the trouble to spend some extra "quality time" with each one. You get the drift . . .

Loving God, thank you for making me an "embodied spirit," and help me to care for both as one. Amen.

If only we try to live sincerely, it will go well with us, even though we are certain to experience real sorrow, and great disappointments, and shall also probably commit great errors and do wrong things; but it certainly is true that it is better to be high-spirited, even though one makes more mistakes, than to be narrow-minded and overprudent.

— VINCENT VAN GOGH,
The Complete Letters of Vincent van Gogh

LENT, LENT, OH LENT, come over here and sit down for a minute. Tell me, Lent, what is your secret? You can trust me...I'm listening, yes. What? That's your secret, that the secret of life is to live sincerely. As your servant Vincent said, to live sincerely? Sincerity, that's it? But is it not possible for misguided or bad people to be sincere in the evil they do? Tell me, Lent. Explain, please...

It is not possible for a truly sincere person to have a dark or evil heart. To be sincere requires a good heart, honesty, lack of guile. Above all, sincerity requires simplicity of heart. There is truth in a sincere person, the truth that he or she seeks the good of others first and foremost.

Of course, sincere thoughts and sincere behavior do not rule out sorrow, as Vincent said. Neither does it guarantee success. A sincere person may make big mistakes, hurt other people, make the worst choice instead of the best choice. Sincerity, in other words, does not neutralize our "fallen" condition. No. Lent puts an arm around your shoulder, gives you a sideways hug, and encourages you to be broad-minded and take some chances. Don't be "over-prudent," as Vincent said.

Vincent, oh Vincent. You were one of the world's most sincere people, and you were a genius, and your paintings are both heart-breaking and enough to make a person laugh out

12

loud with joy. But you knew that true sincerity is not narrow-minded and is willing to stick its neck out for the right reason. Then it will go well with us.

God of Lent, thank you for helping me to take
some risks based on faith and trust in you;
help me to act with sincerity in all that I do. Amen.

Monday, First Week of Lent

About the Ignatian method of meditation: it sounds fine but I can't do it. I am no good at meditating. This doesn't mean that I get right on with contemplating. I don't do either. If I attempt to keep my mind on the mysteries of the rosary, I am soon thinking about something else, entirely non-religious in nature. So I read my prayers out of the book, prime in the morning and compline at night.
— FLANNERY O'CONNOR, *The Habit of Being*

WE WANT LIFE to be soft as an easy chair and comfy as can be. We whine and complain if life throws us a curve, if we find that our usual song and dance does not spare us from suffering. Flannery O'Connor, a young Catholic writer of fiction, Georgia born and bred, faced life and suffering squarely, with grace, with patience, with humor even. She said that she could only pray as she could pray, and that's how she prayed.

Flannery O'Connor faced suffering — she had lupus before medical science could do much about it — with nothing more than a desire to write her stories and share her stories. When she felt bad she said so, but then she let it drop. Self-pity was not her style.

Imagine in the midst of our troubles thinking of nothing more than trying to share our gifts, talents, small efforts, with those around us. Imagine Lent as a time to do that. Imagine trying not to be afraid, no matter what happens to us. Imagine doing that. If we can imagine it, we can do it. For if we act as if we have faith we will have faith, and if we act as if we have hope and love we will have hope and love. Imagine that.

> God of love and courage, thank you for the example
> of people like Flannery O'Connor, who help us
> to live with more faith and more joy. Amen.

❊   Tuesday, First Week of Lent   ❊

> *I entered within [myself] and saw, with my soul's eye (such as it was), an unchangeable light. It was shining above the eye of my soul and above my mind, not that ordinary light visible to all flesh nor something of the same kind, only greater as though it might be ordinary light shining more brightly and with its greatness filling all things. Your light was not that kind but another kind, utterly different from all these.*

> — SAINT AUGUSTINE OF HIPPO, *Confessions*

SAY THIS: "God lives in me." Say it again. Now say this: "God lives in the people I love the most." Say it again. Then say this: "God lives in every person I will meet today." Now say it again.

We are in God and God is in us. All of us together. There is no separation from God's love, only a forgetting, a lack of mindfulness, or indifference, or distraction. We can forget about God but God never forgets about us. The universe sings with the love of God, and God fills all the vast outer reaches of space, and God lives in you, God lives in you.

We say these words, and we believe what we say. In our heart we do believe what we say. But our actions, what about our actions? What about the way we go about a typical day?

Do our actions say what we say to ourselves? Say God — the Creator of the Universe, the Ground of All Being, the Great Cosmic Wherewithal, Absolutely Unconditional Love — lives in a person. What difference might that make in a person's attitudes, feelings, outlook on life, relationships with other people? What difference might that make in how a person does his or her work? Maybe then we should see some of these differences in ourselves if God lives in us.

If we are mindful of God in us, if we are mindful, then we may not see these differences in ourselves, but other people will. Other people will. If we are mindful of God in us.

Loving Father, help me to turn to you many times throughout the day, to be mindful of your love for me and for all the people I meet every day. Amen.

Wednesday, First Week of Lent

I was reminded of a story Mother Clark up at the Cenacle of St. Regis had told me of a little girl who was being instructed for her First Holy Communion. They were asking her what a spirit was and when she could not answer they started asking her questions.

"Has a spirit got eyes or hair?"

"Has a spirit arms or legs?" And so on.

She agreed that a spirit had none of these things but she finally said brightly:

"But a spirit has feathers!"

— Dorothy Day, *Meditations*

WE FIND IT TOUGH to think of a spirit. Is a spirit like a little balloon of gas floating around? Angels are spirits, but in order to think of an angel we think of the traditional image of a figure of indeterminate sex with large feathery wings. In other words, we can't think of an angel without using a bodily image of an angel. The wings are there as a sign of the angel's spiritual nature and ability to travel with the speed of thought.

Because we are embodied spirits ourselves, we can't think of a spirit without a body. This is how important our bodies are to us. What would we do without them? Yet how often do we think of our body as having spiritual significance? Our poor bodies, are they just along for the ride? We use them, abuse them, and wear them out, then cast them aside? We enjoy our body and suffer from our body, tolerate our body and drag it around until we die?

Maybe there is more to it than that. The Son of God became fully human, just like us, body and all. So there must be something glorious about being a bodily being, not just a pure spirit...whatever that may be. If a body was good enough for Jesus, it's good enough for us.

Lord God, thank you for the grace of being an embodied spirit; help me to respect and care for my bodiliness as a special gift from you. Amen.

※　　　**Thursday, First Week of Lent**　　　※

Is it not so? is not Scripture altogether pleasant except in its strictness? do not we try to persuade ourselves, that to feel religiously, to confess our love of religion, and to be able to talk of religion, will stand in the place of careful obedience, of that self-denial which is the very substance of true practical religion? Alas! that religion which is so delightful as a vision, should be so distasteful as a reality. Yet so it is, whether we are aware of the fact or not.

— JOHN HENRY NEWMAN, *Parochial and Plain Sermons*

16

I N HIS NOVEL *Burning Angel* author James Lee Burke has a low-life scoundrel make a kind of secular confession about having pushed a Mennonite missionary out of a helicopter over a Central American jungle. As the low-life did so, the woman looked directly in his eyes. She said, *"You must change your way."*

This is what scripture and our faith insist upon, that we must change our way. Faith is based on a personal relationship with God, the Divine Mystery, the Ground of All Being, the Great Cosmic Wherewithal. Faith hits us where we live. We feel our faith, we think about our faith, and we act on our faith. So we are to change in all these ways.

Sometimes we think that our religion is to make us feel better when the going gets rough, and there is some truth to that. Sometimes we think that our religion is about what will happen to us after we buy the farm, and there is some truth to that. Sometimes we think that our religion is about loving God and neighbor here and now, and there is much truth to that.

Fact is, the Christian religion is about all of these but it's about something even more fundamental than any of them. It's about God's love for us, a love that is unconditional, absolute, and completely reliable. Because God's love is so reliable our religion calls us to change our way. We need act on fear and anxiety no longer, only on trust.

Lord Jesus, help me to face up to my religion as more
than a comfort, as a challenge that can be difficult
and demanding and is meant to be so. Amen.

Friday, First Week of Lent

Not long ago a very learned man told me that souls who do
not practice prayer are like people with paralyzed or crippled
bodies; even though they have hands and feet they cannot

*give orders to these hands and feet. Thus there are souls so
ill and so accustomed to being involved in external matters
that there is no remedy, nor does it seem that they can enter
within themselves.*

— SAINT TERESA OF AVILA, *The Interior Castle*

HERE'S A TOUGH ONE. We know we should pray, and we do
pray. We are convinced that we do not pray enough. Too
busy. Too much going on. Places to go, people to see, things
to do. We are like the White Rabbit in Lewis Carroll's *Alice
in Wonderland:* "I'm late, I'm late, for a very important date!"
Off we dash, down our own personal rabbit hole of daily activities, only to surface at night when we're too exhausted to
see straight.

So who has enough time for prayer? Lent is a good time,
a good time indeed, to think about this. We need prayer. But
we think we don't have enough time to pray as we should.
Maybe we need to ask ourselves what prayer is. Let's not get
too complicated. To pray is to become aware of God's presence in and all around us. Prayer is awareness first, words or
thoughts second. Awareness of God's presence, that's prayer
and that's what we hang our words on.

So we can pray any time, any place, any how. Here is when
you can pray: while waiting for the traffic light to change;
while waiting for the water to boil; while riding a bus, sub-
way, or train; while riding a bicycle or riding a hot-air balloon;
in the middle of a walk in the middle of a city; as you switch
the laundry from the washer to the drier or hang it on the line;
during a coffee break or in the middle of a conundrum; when
you are sad and when you are happy.

To pray is to turn your thoughts to God, no matter what
else is going on. To pray is to know that you are loved by God
no matter what. Now, if this is prayer how often do you pray?
More often than you thought?

Lord Jesus, help me to have a deeper appreciation for how often I pray each and every day. Amen.

Saturday, First Week of Lent

You must not be astonished when, even at the risk of your taking me for a fanatic, I tell you that in order to love, I think it absolutely necessary to believe in God...; to me, to believe in God is to feel that there is a God, not dead or stuffed but alive, urging us to love again with irresistible force — that is my opinion.

— Vincent van Gogh,
The Complete Letters of Vincent van Gogh

WHAT DOES IT MEAN to love? The word "love" has many meanings in our culture. Sometimes it has self-centered meanings, meanings that sparkle like a Las Vegas casino, loaded with glitz, but meanings that are as dead as a doornail. The only love that holds water, that is reliable and lasting is the love Saint Thomas Aquinas described seven hundred years ago. He said that to love is to will the good of the other. To will the good of the other person is to will our own good, as well.

We think of love as an emotion that feels good. Bubbly. Sometimes this is true, and we should thank God for such times. Most of the time, however, love does not feel particularly good. Love is what gets us out of bed in the morning to work at a job we may not like for the sake of those we love. Love is the will to love that keeps a married couple together, the choice to intend the good of the other as one's own good.

In such a love we find God, a living God, not a God who is "dead or stuffed" but a living God who urges us to love and go on loving time after time, again and again. God is love, therefore to love is to be in God and to have God in us.

19

It's a great mystery. Because God is love and God loves us, God is in us already. But when we choose to love we discover the truth of God's presence in us. It's a great mystery.

God of Lent, thank you for the gift of your presence in me
and in all the people I encounter today;
help me to love them as you love them. Amen.

✖ Second Sunday of Lent ✖

I have 50 or 60 pages [written] on the [new] novel but I
still expect to be a long time at it. It's a theme that requires
prayer and fasting to make it get anywhere. I manage to
pray but am a very sloppy faster.
— FLANNERY O'CONNOR, *The Habit of Being*

LENT IS A TIME for prayer and fasting, but most of us are rather sloppy at it. We manage a prayer here and there, and we do a middling job of fasting according to the traditions of Lent. Maybe we "give up" something for Lent. Usually what we give up is something we like that is maybe bad for us in the first place, which is fine — candy, desserts, caffeine, alcohol, nicotine, that sort of thing. But look. Look.

Lent is a time to grow deeper, not just "give up" something that isn't particularly good for us to begin with. What is the goal of our prayer and fasting, such as it is? To become a deeper person, a more loving, caring, compassionate person. To become more Christ-like. That's the purpose of Lent and the purpose of our prayer and fasting. Such as it is.

But there can be more to Lent. Say we have a concern. Say we're worried about one of our children or one of our grandchildren, or we want to accomplish something creative. Prayer and fasting can be forms of prayer to help us empty ourselves to make room for God to influence our efforts or have an impact on the source of our concern. We pray and we fast, such as it is, and thus allow ourselves to be more open to God's will and God's action in our life and the lives of those we love.

We pray and fast imperfectly, of course. We are sloppy fasters. But we know that God's love and power does not depend on our fasting or our praying. We do what we can and that's good enough. God takes care of the rest. And that's good enough.

God our loving Father, thank you for helping me to do
what praying and fasting I can do during Lent;
help me to let that be good enough. Amen.

❈ Monday, Second Week of Lent ❈

And I observed other things and discerned that they owe
their being to you [O Lord], and that all finite things are in
you, but differently, not as in space but because you are and
hold all things in the hand of your truth . . . And I observed
that all things harmonized not only with their places but also
with their times . . .

— SAINT AUGUSTINE OF HIPPO, *Confessions*

WE LIVE AND BREATHE this notion that there is a great gulf between God and us, between the sacred and the secular, the holy and the profane. But this is not true, not true at all. Saint Paul says that we "live and move and have our being" in God (Acts 17:28). The Second Letter of Peter declares that we are "participants of the divine nature" (1:4), which means — brace yourself — that God's nature is part of our nature.

There is no vast gulf between us and God, between the holy and the ordinary. We are in God, and God lives in us. Therefore, God is everyplace, even places that seem devoid of anything having to do with God. God is there, ready to break through at the slightest invitation. God is in the sunshine, but God is in the darkness, too. God hates pain and suffering more than we do — but God is present even in pain and suffering because God's own Son accepted pain and suffering himself.

It's all a mystery, of course. Mystery within mystery within mystery, and in the end all is joy. All is joy in the end because this life is brief and our ultimate destiny, beyond this life, is eternal joy. Mystery within mystery within mystery, and in the end God's love is all.

This is the stuff of silent loving prayer. Sit still, breathe evenly, close your eyes or open your eyes, bask in God's loving presence in you, and all around you, and in all that your day will bring.

Loving God, thank you for the gift of your presence in me, and thank you for the gift of all things present in you. Amen.

Tuesday, Second Week of Lent

One day last summer, I saw a man sitting down by one of the piers, all alone. He sat on a log, and before him was a wooden box on which he had spread out on a paper his meager supper. He sat there and ate with some pretense of human dignity, and it was one of the saddest sights I have ever seen.

— DOROTHY DAY, *Meditations*

WE THINK OF LENT as a time to eat less, not more. But as we eat less what difference does it make? What difference does it make for us and for others? To fast, to eat less, is to deny the self. We don't fast because God disapproves of food or the pleasure of eating. We fast as a way to "unself" ourself.

In Matthew's Gospel Jesus announces: "Woe to you, scribes

and Pharisees, hypocrites! For you clean the outside of the cup and of the plate, but inside they are full of greed and self-indulgence" (23:25). This is the point, of course: self-indulgence. We fast in order to loose the chains that bind us to the self. By fasting we make room in our heart for God and we make room for other people. We shift the focus from self to God and neighbor.

Of course, fasting can also be an exercise in sympathy. To feel empty voluntarily may help us to sympathize with the countless people in the world who feel empty because they have no other choice. To be a little hungry for a little while is to get some inkling of what it feels like to be hungry big-time all the time.

Fasting is an exercise in freedom, freedom from slavery to our appetite for food, freedom from our inclination to indulge ourselves, freedom from our inclination to focus on the self to the neglect of God and neighbor. And in this freedom there is a deep and quiet joy.

Loving God, help me to practice the light fasting of Lent with a light and peaceful spirit. Amen.

Wednesday, Second Week of Lent

We read a passage in the Gospels . . . a parable perhaps, or the account of a miracle; or we read a chapter in the Prophets, or a Psalm. Who is not struck with the beauty of what he reads? I do not wish to speak of those who read the Bible only now and then, and who will in consequence generally find its sacred pages dull and uninteresting; but of those who study it. Who of such persons does not see the beauty of it?

— John Henry Newman, *Parochial and Plain Sermons*

ARE YOU A SEEKER? Do you search for meaning, deeper meaning in life, in *your* life? Do you wonder about the purpose of it all? Answers aplenty float around out there. Maybe people knock on your door ready to give you the answers. Maybe Television Personalities are ready with no end of answers. Maybe bookstore and library shelves are loaded with psychological techniques and whiz-bangs from a New Age perspective.

Sometimes we overlook the most obvious sources of insight because we have Funny Feelings about them. Take the Bible. It has a sanctimonious reputation. It's "the Good Book." It's "the Holy Bible." It's "churchy." It's filled with ancient, otherworldly prose with no connection to my ordinary, everyday, knockabout life...

But no. Grab a paperback Bible. Pick it up like any paperback book. Find a used, beaten, dog-eared copy. Do whatever you need to do to rid yourself of sanctimonious preconceptions. Flip the pages. Toss it in a corner and neglect it for a few days. Then...slowly, casually, sneak up on it in an off moment. Sidle up to it, pick it up, open it with an open mind and an open heart, expecting nothing but ready for anything.

Say something to the question in your heart, the question at the center of your being. Say something like, "Hello, I'm here and I'm searching. I want to find some answers. I want to see your face." Then browse slowly through your dog-eared Bible. Chances are that in a few minutes you will want to kiss the words you read. Chances are...

God of the question at the center of my being,
thank you for leading me into your marvelous light;
help me to find you. Amen.

Well, if we never look at Him, or reflect on what we owe Him and the death He suffered for us, I don't know how we'll be able to know or do works in His service. And what value can faith have without works and without joining them to the merits of Jesus Christ, our God? Or who will awaken us to love this Lord?

— SAINT TERESA OF AVILA, *The Interior Castle*

FAITH CAN BE such a "head trip." If we allow it to be so, faith can be a "head trip" and-a-half. Thing is, thing is, faith is not supposed to be a "head trip." Faith is supposed to be a "heart trip." A "head trip" we can be very objective about, even impersonal and analytical. A "heart trip," on the other hand, we can't be objective about. It's a matter of love, and it's a matter of action. When you love you can't sit still. When you love you act on your love. You do something about it.

Here is what love does: it changes your life. When you love you can't go on living the way you lived before. You change your ways. Your values change, for what matters now is what you love. You act on your love, giving the person or cause you love your best energies and the best hours of your day.

Faith, sometimes, is another word for love. To have Christian faith is to have a close personal relationship with Christ. Because you love him and dedicate yourself to him, you act on his behalf and on behalf of all his people. This love goes hand-in-hand with works of faith: caring for and serving others. Caring for and serving those closest to us, first. Then we throw wide our arms to embrace and care for all the world.

Impossible, you say? But no. Because we are "in Christ" his love is our love, and his love knows no limits, no boundaries, nothing small or self-contained. His love is our love and it embraces all the world.

*Loving Christ, thank you for the opportunity to love
both locally and globally; help me to respond faithfully
and with joy. Amen.*

※   **Friday, Second Week of Lent**   ※

*But if one feels the need of something grand, something infi-
nite, something that makes one feel aware of God, one need
not go far to find it. I think I see something deeper, more
infinite, more eternal than the ocean in the expression of the
eyes of a little baby when it wakes in the morning, and coos
and laughs because it sees the sun shining on its cradle. If
there is a "ray from on high," perhaps one can find it there.*

— VINCENT VAN GOGH,
The Complete Letters of Vincent van Gogh

IF WE'RE NOT CAREFUL Lent can seem to be a "churchy"
season. With a cockeyed perspective like this Lent becomes
real for us only on the six Sundays of Lent — in church.
Rather, Lent is an every-day-for-forty-days affair. But if Lent
is an everyday reality what does it have to do with everyday
concerns?

For Lent we may "give up" our inclination to think of only
churchy things as holy. We can work on seeing the sacred everyplace. We can snap our eyes open to the holiness of the
ordinary. We can see the eternal in the eyes of a baby ... or in
the eyes of a potato. We can see the infinite in a grain of sand
and the face of God in a clear night sky.

More than this, we can work on seeing the holy in the ordinary activities of our everyday life. It's holy to climb out of bed
in the morning and go to work, whether we enjoy our work or
not, because we do it for our family. It's holy to help children
with their homework, and it's holy to attend a parent/teacher
conference. It's holy to prepare a meal, and it's holy to clean a

bathroom or vacuum the carpets. It's holy to ask your spouse about his or her day and really listen to the response. It's holy to make love with your spouse, and it's holy to work through conflict with your spouse when you would rather not. It's holy to be friendly with the clerk at the supermarket, and it's holy to be patient with a teenager.

Holiness is here, there, and everywhere, and God is in the most unremarkable moments.

Lord God, thank you for being in all the ordinary times; help me to see you more clearly there. Amen.

❋ Saturday, Second Week of Lent ❋

I think that the reason such Catholics are so repulsive is that they don't really have faith but a kind of false certainty. They operate by the slide rule and the Church for them is not the body of Christ but a poor man's insurance system. It's never hard for them to believe because actually they never think about it.

— FLANNERY O'CONNOR, *The Habit of Being*

HARD WORDS, a harsh saying. But true for all that. Do we have authentic faith or "a kind of false certainty"? Is faith for us a spiritual security blanket, a "poor man's insurance system"? It's a hard question, a splash of cold water in the face, spiritually speaking. But an important question to face up to for all that.

Lent is the best time, of all times, to purify our faith. Fact is, faith is a source of security only if it first leads to *in*security. A faith that takes no risks is hardly faith at all. Now *this* is a harsh truth. We of all people cling to every source of security — economic security in particular — we can lay our hands on. We take no chances we don't need to take. We advise our children to do the same. A penny saved is a penny earned. A bird in the hand is worth two in the bush. Leave well enough alone. Don't stick your neck out.

Genuine faith, on the contrary, prompts us to take chances. Faith also requires us to think about our faith. When was the last time I read a book that helped me to think about the meaning of my faith? When was the last time I thought about some of the hard questions faith must face up to in today's world? What impact does my faith have on my marriage, my role as a parent, my work, how I use my leisure time, my daily life in general, my political views?

If I think about my faith, think about it seriously, there should be times when it's not easy to believe. There should be such times.

Lord God, thank you for the gift of faith;
help me to accept the risks faith sometimes requires. Amen.

Third Sunday of Lent

How sweet it suddenly became for me to be without the sweetness of trifling things! And how glad I was to give up the things that I had been so afraid to lose! For you cast them out, O true and highest Sweetness, and you entered into me to take their place, sweeter than all pleasure, though not to flesh and blood; brighter than all light, but more hidden within than any secret thing. . . . And I was conversing like a child to you, to my Brightness, my Wealth, and my Salvation, my Lord God.

— Saint Augustine of Hippo, *Confessions*

LENT IN A NUTSHELL. To give up self by setting aside, at least for a time, the sweetness of things that are — in the long run — trifling things. Oh, but we are such babies about it sometimes. We are afraid to lose the sweetness of trifling things. We whimper at the thought of losing a few small pleasures or comforts for a mere month, and a week, and a few more days. We whine about it not because we will miss our trifling sweetness, our little pleasure or comfort — though we may think that this is it — but because in losing these things for a time we fear that we will, in the process, lose ourself.

But this is just the point — to lose myself, to die to myself, to empty myself, make space in myself for God and neighbor to come in. By fasting and abstinence for Lent we push back the clutter in our soul, sweep out a corner, so there is a bit more emptiness for God and neighbor to take up residence. Of course, we don't have to do the emptying. Our loving God will do that. If we ask. If we but ask.

We may be surprised to find that a bit more emptiness is not an empty feeling but a feeling sweeter than all the sweetness we knew before. God becomes, a bit more, our Brightness, our Wealth, our Salvation, our Lord God.

God our loving Father, thank you for the gift of more
emptiness during Lent; fill my emptiness
with your own unutterable Fullness. Amen.

Monday, Third Week of Lent

Our lives are made up of little miracles day by day. That splendid globe of sun, one street wide, framed at the foot of East 14th Street in early morning mists, that greeted me on my way out to Mass was a miracle that lifted up my heart.

— Dorothy Day, *Meditations*

It's trite to say that everything is a miracle, or each day is filled with little miracles. It's trite, but it's also as true as true can be. Our days are filled with miracles we miss by a mile. Sometimes it's good to sit ourselves down, or stand ourselves up, and turn ourselves around, and make the effort to see the miracles right in front of us. Sometimes it's good to start close to home. Sometimes it's good to start with ourselves.

Open your eyes and look. Look at yourself in a mirror. What do you see? You see the same face you see every morning in the mirror. But stop. Take a closer look. Here's the thing. What you see is a miracle. There you stand, ordinary you with your face hanging out. There you stand, ordinary you. But notice. Your eyes are open; you breathe in and out; you live and move and have your being. Do you do this? Do you keep your heart going, thumping in your chest? It's a miracle, isn't it?

It's a miracle. You are a miracle that you overlook most of the time. The Creator of the universe keeps you going, your eyes open, your heart thumping in your chest. You may have some handicap, perhaps you move about in a wheelchair, but you are alive, your heart carries on, your spirit carries on. It's a miracle you mostly overlook.

Praise the God who works the miracle. Quietly, quietly, praise the God who keeps you in existence, who holds you in the palm of his hand. Now and forever. Praise.

Lord God, thank you for the miracle of myself;
help me to think of this miracle more often
and thank you for it more often. Amen.

Tuesday, Third Week of Lent

[Christ] says, "I will take away from you the heart of stone . . . if you will submit to My discipline." Here a man draws back. No . . . he cannot consent to be changed. After all he

is well satisfied at the bottom of his heart to remain as he is,
only he wants his conscience taken out of the way.
— JOHN HENRY NEWMAN, *Parochial and Plain Sermons*

THERE IS MUCH about the spiritual life that is hilarious once we stop to think about it. Good for a chuckle or two — at our expense, of course, for we are the goofy ones. We say to the Lord God, the Creator of the Universe, the God of Abraham and Sarah, Isaac and Rebekah, Jacob and Rachel, we say: "Change my heart, make of me a faithful follower of Christ." And so on and so forth. "Lord Jesus Christ, Son of God, have mercy on me, a sinner." And what have you. But it's all a bluff.

The Lord Jesus would gladly change our heart, make it no longer a heart of stone, give us a heart ready to love and be loved . . . but we really would rather not. When we're up against the wall what we want is what we want, not what God wants. We admire the example of the saints but we would prefer not to become one ourselves. We would like to have a reputation for holiness or virtue, oh yes. But we would not like to give up what we would have to give up in order to be truly holy or virtuous. No, no, no, none of that.

We don't believe that to give up our own will, wishes, desires, preferences, and visible sources of security would leave us open to God's gift of the most overwhelming freedom, joy, and peace. We say we believe it, but we do not, because we want what we want, and that's the end of that.

Lord God of love, thank you for the gift
of spiritual healing and liberation;
help me to know in my heart that your mercy
is trustworthy beyond all things. Amen.

It is a great misery to have to live a life in which we must always walk like those whose enemies are at their doorstep; they can neither sleep nor eat without weapons and without being always frightened lest somewhere these enemies might be able to break through this fortress.

— SAINT TERESA OF AVILA, *The Interior Castle*

WORRY AND FEAR, worry and fear, and anxiety is a way of life. How we worry. How we fear that something terrible may happen to us. What if this happens? What if that happens? The wolf is at the door and the worst is to be expected. This is how we live so much of the time; this is how we live.

But Jesus has other ideas, and the gospel is about another way of life. The Jesus of the Gospels knows the human heart like the back of his hand, and he has other ideas. Over and over, time after time, with quiet insistence he urges his disciples to stop being afraid, to stop being anxious and fearful. Over and over, time after time, with quiet insistence he urges his disciples to abandon fear and trust in God's love. Over and over, time after time, he recommends another way of life.

When we worry that something terrible might happen, could happen, Jesus speaks to us the words he speaks to the leader of the synagogue in Mark's Gospel: "Do not fear, only believe" (Mk 5:36). These are good words, words worthy of trust. But even when something terrible *does* happen, Jesus speaks the same words to us: "Do not fear, only believe."

Can we do this? Can we give up fear and only believe, even when something terrible does happen? Can we? We need not pretend. If we don't feel that we can have such trust we can simply make this our prayer. Lord, I do believe but help my unbelief. This we can do no matter what.

God our loving Father, thank you for the gift of faith
and trust in you; help me to abandon myself completely
to your love — no matter what. Amen.

❈ Thursday, Third Week of Lent ❈

Just as we take the train to get to Tarascon or Rouen, we
take death to reach a star. . . .
  So to me it seems possible that cholera, gravel, tubercu-
losis and cancer are the celestial means of locomotion, just
as steamboats, buses and railways are the terrestrial means.
To die quietly of old age would be to go there on foot.

— VINCENT VAN GOGH,
The Complete Letters of Vincent van Gogh

IN THE OLD DAYS, Christians pondered death a good deal, especially during Lent. Lent was a season of intense pon-derables, dark thoughts of dust and to dust you shall return. No weddings during Lent. No merry-making during Lent. A season of spiritual gloom before the explosion of fire and light at the Easter Vigil.

In the Old Days, Christians pondered death. We, in our enlightened state, may consider this morbid. What? Think of death? Isn't faith about life? Death? How depressing. But there's a mental switch-back here that we may be missing, and if we miss it we may miss the Big Picture. Can we know life without facing death? Perhaps not, oh, perhaps not at all.

Fact is, we kid ourselves. Big time. We avoid thoughts of mortality and death not because we believe so deeply in life and resurrection. We avoid thoughts of dusty death because . . . we are naturally terrified by it. What makes us dif-ferent from people in the Old Days is that we kid ourselves about it while they faced up to it, looked death in the eye.

33

Sometimes they went too far, became morbid about it. But that doesn't justify our game of make believe.

Lent is still a good time to think about death. The old question: If this were the last day of your life on this earth how would you live it?

God of life, thank you for the gift of life and the gift of mortality; help me to live this day inspired by your Spirit in all that I do, even the most ordinary things. Amen.

Friday, Third Week of Lent

In fact I seem to have nothing but friends who have left the Church. They have all left because they have been shocked by the intellectual dishonesty of some Catholic or other... It's only partly that but it does account for a good deal. I wish we would hear more preaching about the harm we do from the things we do not face and from all the questions that we give Instant Answers to.

— FLANNERY O'CONNOR, *The Habit of Being*

FRIENDS who have left the church, adult offspring who have left the church, aunts, uncles, cousins and shirt-tail relations who have left the church. So many, it seems. It can be a heart-breaker. Why do they leave? How can they abandon their spiritual roots with such apparent ease? If they left the church because a priest was rude to them, or some official church teaching offended them, do they not know that the church is not one priest or a certain — in all likelihood non-infallible — teaching? If they can find a perfect church, or a perfect world, they should go ahead and join it, but as soon as they do, it won't be perfect anymore...

Why do we expect the church to be perfect *according to our standards of perfection?* The people who make up the church are imperfect, sinful human beings, and we shouldn't be surprised to discover this time and again. But the church is also the body of Christ, one, holy, catholic and apostolic.

At the same time, we must ask ourselves if we have given Instant Answers when someone had some difficulty or doubt related to the church. Or do we allow people to be searchers, to ask honest questions and have honest doubts? Do we encourage them to find God precisely in their questions and their doubts?

Loving God, thank you for being present in the darkness as well as in the light; help me to be open to your love and grace in both situations. Amen.

Saturday, Third Week of Lent

Who am I and what am I? What evil have I not done in my acts, or, if not in my acts, in my words, or if not in my words, then in my will? But you, O Lord, are good and merciful, and you looked helpfully upon the depth of my death, and from the bottom of my heart you emptied out the sea of corruption with your right hand. And this was what your hand did: I was able totally to turn from what I willed and to will what you willed.

— Saint Augustine of Hippo, *Confessions*

We live in interesting times, remarkable times. Time was, we were all "sinners." Now we have "low self-esteem." Time was, we deserved punishment for our sins. Now when we do something bad it's not our fault, it's our parents' fault. Time was, people craved "redemption" or "salvation." Now people want to get in touch with "the child within."

Modern psychology, even some of the pop psychology that spawns endless self-help books, has some legitimate insights.

No question about that. But there comes a point where conditioning, the effects of a less than ideal childhood, comes to an end and our own free choices kick into gear. At some point we need to stop blaming other people — our parents, our siblings, our teachers, "the priests," "the nuns," "society" — for our troubles, and start taking responsibility for ourselves. If I am miserable as an adult it does no good to whine about being victimized by my parents or teachers when I was growing up. The past is the past, the present is all I have to work with, and it's time to pick myself up and get on with my life.

To one degree or another we are sinners. But to an unlimited degree God's love is greater than all our sins. Our God is closer to us than we are to ourselves, and his love brings freedom and healing.

God our loving Father, thank you for the gift
of your saving, healing love in Christ;
help me to open myself to that love always. Amen.

✳ Fourth Sunday of Lent ✳

But now our cash box is empty. We just collected the last pennies for a ball of twine and stamps and we shall take a twenty-five-cent subscription [to The Catholic Worker*] which just came in to buy meat for a stew for supper. But the printing bill, the one hundred and sixty-five dollars of it which remains unpaid, confronts us and tries to intimidate us.*

But what is one hundred and sixty-five dollars to St. Joseph, or to St. Teresa of Avila either? We refuse to be affrighted.

Don Bosco tells lots of stories about needing this sum or that sum to pay rent and other bills with and the money

36

arriving miraculously on time. And he too was always in
need, always asking, and always receiving.

— DOROTHY DAY, Meditations

PICK UP any recently published book on the saints, or flip through the pages of a collection of prayers and find the ones with saints' names in the titles. Most likely you will find little if anything on *praying to* the saints. Writers hold up saints as good examples, models of holiness, and so forth. But the idea of praying to the saints, asking for their intercession, for their prayers on our behalf, what has happened to this ancient tradition? Was it overdone in the past, or abused, so now we move to the other extreme and hardly ever pray to a favorite saint?

The idea of prayer to saints goes back to the earliest days of the Christian community. We ask for their prayers, we don't worship them in place of God. We have the old tradition, for example, of praying to Saint Anthony of Padua for help when something is lost. We have, for example, the more recent tradition — only since the 1930s — of praying to Saint Jude Thaddeus in seemingly hopeless situations. We pray to God and we ask the saint to join his or her prayers to ours.

What a team, the saints and us, praying up a storm.

Loving God, thank you for giving us friends in heaven
to pray for us; help me to rely more often on their prayers
as I pray that your will be done. Amen.

✖   Monday, Fourth Week of Lent   ✖

You must know that you can do nothing of yourself; your
past experience has taught you this; therefore look to God
for the will and the power; ask Him earnestly in His Son's

name; seek His holy ordinances. Is not this in your power?
Have you not power at least over the limbs of your body,
so as to attend the means of grace constantly? Have you
literally not the power to come hither; to observe the Fasts
and Festivals of the Church; to come to His Holy Altar and
receive the bread of life?

— JOHN HENRY NEWMAN, *Parochial and Plain Sermons*

A PREACHER'S VOICE rings down through the decades from the mid-19th century, and the words are not words you would hear from a pulpit in a church today. The words are those of a man who believed that people have no hope apart from God's love. Imagine that. Newman didn't give homilies, he preached. And he preached with a power that did not come from himself. He took for granted that people are inclined to be spiritual namby-pambys, which is true. Today it is as true as it was in Newman's time.

Poor me. Whine, whimper, whine. I am a victim, and I am without power or control. Buck up, Newman whispers from his place in an English pulpit more than a hundred years ago. Stiff upper lip and all that. You have more control over yourself and your situation than you think you do. Attend to God's "ordinances" — an old-timey term meaning not only the laws of God, above all the law of love — but meaning, also, the customs, traditions, and rites and rituals of Catholicism. Attend to "the means of grace." Eucharist and Reconciliation/Confession, by all means and always. The customs of Lent, the fasting and abstinence, by all means.

But other, more everyday "means of grace" are vital, too. Making more time to listen and talk to each other is a source of grace for a married couple. More frequently during Lent. Imagine that. A few minutes of daily prayer with scripture is a source of grace. Less television can definitely be a means of grace. Listen more attentively, more often, to a child. Give away something you cherish to someone you cherish. The possibilities are endless . . .

Loving Father, thank you for the sources of grace all around me; help me to take greater advantage of them day by day. Amen.

❊ ## Tuesday, Fourth Week of Lent ❊

Let us look at our own faults and leave aside those of others . . . Perhaps we could truly learn from the one who shocks us what is most important even though we may surpass him in external composure and our way of dealing with others. Although good, these latter things are not what is most important; nor is there any reason to desire that everyone follow at once our own path, or to set about teaching the way of the spirit to someone who perhaps doesn't know what such a thing is.
— SAINT TERESA OF AVILA, *The Interior Castle*

ON THE ONE HAND, there is what we think being a Christian is about. On the other hand, there is the truth of the matter. Inevitably, our vision of the gospel, of the Christian life, of what it means to be a good Catholic, is too narrow. We have it figured out, in a neat package, tied up with a bow. Then along comes someone who startles us, perhaps scandalizes us, and it is from that person that we learn how narrow our vision was.

Imagine learning something about what it means to be a good Christian from someone who believes that abortion is acceptable. Imagine being inspired by someone's charitable or courageous actions. Then later we learn that he or she rarely attends formal religious services. Say we have it all figured out, nailed down, what it means to be a good Catholic. Then we learn that one of the most active, inspirational couples in our parish disagrees with our point of view — on birth control, for example.

The deepest spiritual wisdom of Catholicism repeats over and over that we should keep our eyes on our own faults and ignore those of others. There is no room to be judgmental or to condemn others. Leave that to God. No one can look into the privacy of another's relationship with Christ. Take inspiration from the good others do, and overlook what may strike you as a fault or sin. This, deep down, is the way of Jesus the Christ.

Thank you, Lord God, for the gift of the good that others do; help me to trust your mercy concerning my own faults and to ignore the faults of others. Amen.

✖ ## Wednesday, Fourth Week of Lent ✖

Why is religion or justice or art so very holy?
It may well be that people who do nothing but fall in love are more serious and holier than those who sacrifice their love and their hearts to an idea. However this may be, in order to write a book, perform an action, paint a picture in which there is life, one ought to be a live human being oneself.

— VINCENT VAN GOGH,
The Complete Letters of Vincent van Gogh

THE PRIMARY THING, the one thing, is to be alive and live one's life no matter what that life may be. Each person has a life, and that life is holy. Therefore we are to live it as a holy project. Each one gets to be a child, an adolescent, a young adult, and so on, and each one gets to grow old and die. Some, of course, die young, their lives "cut short," we say. But even they had a life that led to another life beyond this life, which is the same for all of us no matter how long our life may be. To live the life we have, that is the goal and the glory of this life.

The main idea behind Christian faith is to be in love — in love with God, in love with other people, living a life dedicated to love. We are not called to sacrifice ourselves for an idea. God is not an idea; rather, God is love. We are called to give our lives for God in service to other people. It's as simple and glorious as that. Imagine such a life and live such a life.

To be truly alive while we are alive, that's the thing. To be a truly live human being. So many wither through worry, anxiety, fear. They stop being truly alive. Every life has difficulties, suffering. But some of the most alive people in the world also suffer the most. Some of the most alive people in the world are dealing with a terminal illness. Some of the least alive people in the world have bodies as healthy as they can be.

Be alive no matter what your circumstances. Be truly alive, that's the ticket.

> God of life and love, thank you for the gift of my life;
> help me to live the unique life you have given me
> and live it to the fullest. Amen.

✖ Thursday, Fourth Week of Lent ✖

The Sisters were so grateful to me for getting their book a publisher that they have presented me with a portable television. I was of course bowled over. One of them had a brother who gave it to her to give me. They don't have money of their own. So me and ma have entered the twentieth century at last. I can now tell you all about Geritol, Pepto-Bismol, Anacin, Bufferin, any kind of soap or floor wax, etc. etc. Fortunately we can get one station which is an educational network and has some interesting things.

41

My nest-watching activities have begun as I have four geese setting.

— FLANNERY O'CONNOR, *The Habit of Being*

TELEVISION is such an all-pervasive presence in our lives that we take it for granted. A television set is no longer a luxury. Most people think of it as a necessity. Even people who say they don't watch much television wouldn't think of not owning a television set. Most households have two or three.

Many people would agree that most television programming is mental pabulum and escapist entertainment. Even the content of news programs is determined by whether it's entertaining or not. Many would agree that the values and attitudes television takes for granted — and so encourages — are frequently at odds with basic Christian values and attitudes. Still... we find it almost impossible to think of living without television.

Television mostly fills us with images that trivialize human life and human relationships and cultivate dissatisfaction with the things we already have. Most of the time it would make more sense to watch geese setting on their eggs.

Loving Father, thank you for the gift of the time of my life; help me to use it wisely. Amen.

Friday, Fourth Week of Lent

Then my mother said: "Son, as for me, I no longer take delight in anything in this life. What I am doing here now, and why I am here I do not know, now that I have nothing else to hope for in this world. There was only one reason why I wanted to remain a little longer in this life, that I should see you a Catholic Christian before I died. This God has granted me superabundantly, for I see you as His servant to the contempt of all worldly happiness."

— SAINT AUGUSTINE, *Confessions*

S OME PARENTS watch their children breeze through adolescence with very few problems with religion, with the church, with attendance at Mass, with their family. Many other parents must suffer through teenage rebellion against anything to do with the church. This is a special form of cross only parents fully understand. Parents know what a difference faith can make in one's life; otherwise, we leave ourselves wide open to being tossed this way and that by influences contrary to the truth. To choose a life that ignores God's presence in us and in the world is to choose an empty life, at best.

Saint Augustine's mother, Monica, prayed for her son for many years and never gave up. Parents today must do the same. If parents pray for their children they need have no fear that their children will ever be apart from God's love and forgiveness. Sometimes parents must allow their children to freely choose to reject the church for a time in order to freely return to it at a later time. For faith freely chosen is the only faith that is truly one's own.

Loving God, thank you for the gift of faith;
please give this same priceless gift to the children
in my life. Amen.

Saturday, Fourth Week of Lent

I am reminded of St. Teresa who said, "The devil sends me so offensive a bad spirit of temper that at times I think I could eat people up."

*I'm glad that she felt that way, too. St. Thomas said
there is no sin in having a righteous wrath provided there is
no undue desire for revenge.*

— DOROTHY DAY, *Meditations*

M ANY PEOPLE have a tough time dealing with anger. It's
the "forbidden emotion." How do I deal with feelings of
anger? What do I get angry about? Children's behavior is a
source of irritation quite often, and sometimes irritation grows
into anger. Later, sometimes we feel guilty about getting angry with a child, not because the anger was inappropriate but
because we said or did things while angry we are ashamed
of later.

Sometimes it's entirely appropriate to be angry with a
child's behavior. The important thing is to make it clear that
nothing can destroy our relationship with the child, our love
for him or her. Nothing.

Sometimes events in the public forum lead to anger. Injustice, apparent acts of stupidity on the part of public officials,
violence, all can be cause for anger. If we didn't feel angry we might not do something to help oppose injustice and
stupidity. In this sense anger is a much more productive emotion than, say, apathy or indifference. Apathy or indifference
can be sinful where anger might be perfectly virtuous. Imagine that.

The important thing is to express our anger in positive,
creative ways. Revenge is never appropriate. Which leads to
heavy questions about how appropriate capital punishment
really is. Really.

*Lord Jesus, thank you for the human emotion of anger;
help me to express my anger in ways consistent
with my loving intimacy with you. Amen.*

...a rigorous self-denial is a chief duty, nay...it may be considered the test whether we are Christ's disciples, whether we are living in a mere dream, which we mistake for Christian faith and obedience, or are really and truly awake, alive, living in the day, on our road heavenwards. The early Christians went through self-denials in their very profession of the Gospel; what are our self-denials, now that the profession of the Gospel is not a self-denial? In what sense do we fulfill the words of Christ? Have we any distinct notion what is meant by the words "taking up our cross"?

— JOHN HENRY NEWMAN, *Parochial and Plain Sermons*

WE LIVE in a society and a culture that couldn't care less what your religious persuasions may be. You can embrace any religion you want, as long as you keep it to yourself. Society views religion as a personal matter, almost a private hobby, that has nothing to do with "the real world." No one will persecute you if you profess faith in Christ. Just don't talk about it at work or in a public school classroom. Don't raise questions based on religious principles at the meeting of your company's board of directors or stockholder's annual meeting. Religion has nothing to do with the real world, you see.

So how do we know our faith is real? How do we know we aren't just cultivating a personal religious fantasy in order to keep anxiety at bay, for example, or in order to seem more socially respectable? How do we know our involvement with the church isn't mainly "for the sake of the children" so they will "get some training in morality"?

Lent is the ideal time to cultivate deeper roots for our faith by self-denial. To deny myself something I like, or to deny myself something that is not good for me that I like all the same, or to deny myself some habit I have that keeps me from a stronger, healthier marriage or friendship, is to act on a faith that is real. To deny myself based on a reality that is invisible — my relationship with Christ — is to say that my faith is not just a pious fiction but the deepest reality there is.

Lord Jesus, thank you for the gift of faith;
help me to deny myself for the sake
of my relationship with you. Amen.

Monday, Fifth Week of Lent

Perhaps we don't know what love is. I wouldn't be very much surprised, because it doesn't consist in great delight but in desiring with strong determination to please God in everything, in striving, insofar as possible, not to offend Him, and in asking Him for the advancement of the honor and glory of His Son and the increase of the Catholic Church. These are the signs of love.

— SAINT TERESA OF AVILA, *The Interior Castle*

WE, OF ALL the people who have ever lived on the earth, have some of the strangest ideas about love. We think first of love as a romantic notion. Someone who is "in love" is thought to be a little crazy but in a nice and pleasant way. Being "in love" is "fun." There is nothing wrong with this understanding. There is something perfectly valid about it, even important. The experience of being "in love" romantically offers a remote hint of the delights of heaven, and we should thank God for it. But this is not all there is of love or even the most important experience of love in this world.

From a Christian point of view, the most real and important kind of love is the love we see in the life, death and Resurrection of Jesus. This is a love that lives and dies for others. This is a love that is willing to seek the good of the other as

46

one's own good. This is why Saint Thomas Aquinas said that to love truly is to will the good of the other. So love, lasting love, deep love, is an act of the will not an effervescent goosey feeling.

At the same time, any experience of love in any form — goosey or not — is an experience of the Divine Mystery. That's why the First Letter of John tells us that "God is love" (4:8). Indeed, all love pleases God and all love makes God present in the world and in the church.

Loving God, thank you for the gift of your presence
as love in my life and in the world;
help me to love as you love in all that I do. Amen.

Tuesday, Fifth Week of Lent

Whence comes it that in the present instance of [my] uncle's death, the face of the deceased was calm, peaceful, and grave, whereas it is a fact that he was rarely that way while living, either in youth or age? . . .

And in the same way a child in the cradle, if you watch it at leisure, has the infinite in its eyes. In short, I know nothing about it, but it is just this feeling of not knowing that makes the real life we are actually living now like a one-way journey on a train. You go fast, but cannot distinguish any object very clearly, and above all you do not see the engine.

— VINCENT VAN GOGH,
The Complete Letters of Vincent van Gogh

THINK ABOUT your average day. Pause for just a few minutes, a few quiet minutes, and think about your average day. You are on the go from the moment you arise, perhaps, until the moment your head hits the pillow at night. Your day

47

is filled with whatever your average day is filled with. Activities of various kinds, perhaps. Your average day is not a quiet, calm, reflective retreat. Hardly.

You go about what you need to go about. But how often do you pause to reflect on what a tremendous, mind-boggling mystery it all is — your life, the world, your life in the world. The mystery of existence, the mystery of other people and your relationships with them. The mystery of the joy and anguish that fills your heart day-in, day-out. The mystery of the sun and the moon and the stars. It's all a great and wonderful mystery, yet so often our eyes are glued to the mundane details. The laundry needs to be done, dinner needs to be planned and prepared, work makes its demands, money needs to be earned and bills must be paid.

All these things are real, but it's important to stop and wonder at the mystery of it all. Now and then it's important to whisper a prayer of gratitude and wonder. Now and then.

Loving Father, thank you for the great mystery of my life and of your creation; help me remember to say thank you from time to time. Amen.

Wednesday, Fifth Week of Lent

I am glad the Church has given you the ability to look at yourself and like yourself as you are. The natural comes before the supernatural and that is perhaps the first step toward finding the Church again. Then you will wonder why it was necessary to look at yourself or like or dislike yourself at all. You will have found Christ when you are concerned with other people's sufferings and not your own.

— FLANNERY O'CONNOR, *The Habit of Being*

OH, A HARD AND DIFFICULT THOUGHT, that having "healthy self-esteem" is but a stepping stone to forgetfulness of self entirely. The popular culture slaps us around daily with the belief that a "healthy self-concept" is an end in itself. Think positive thoughts about yourself, we hear. All this is fine. All this is good. But the Christian ideal goes further than that. The Christian ideal is to keep going beyond healthy self-esteem toward self-forgetfulness for the sake of others.

The "gospel" of the world encourages us to be self-centered in a thousand subtle and sophisticated ways. The gospel of Jesus encourages us to move steadily away from self and toward others. For this we get little support from the popular culture. Don't expect television talk show hosts to encourage this. Don't expect soap operas to celebrate it in the lives of soap opera characters. Don't expect to see messages about it on electronic reader boards. The gospel of Jesus says that we must forget ourselves in order to live, and the world doesn't understand this at all.

We never accomplish this completely, of course, this forgetfulness of self. But the ideal of Jesus is to allow God to move us in this direction. Daily, daily, to move us in this direction.

Lord Jesus, thank you for your gospel which is life and truth; help me to be guided by this gospel day by day. Amen.

✳ Thursday, Fifth Week of Lent ✳

And this is the happy life, to rejoice in you [O Lord] and for you and because of you. This is the happy life, and there is no other. Those who think there is another are pursuing a different joy, which is not the true joy. Nevertheless their will is not utterly turned away from some image of joy.

— SAINT AUGUSTINE OF HIPPO, *Confessions*

GOD'S CREATION and all the marvels dreamed up by the human mind, and fashioned by human hands, can be so captivating in themselves. The earth demands our attention today for it is threatened in many ways. The forests, the grasslands, lakes and rivers, demand our care and respect if they — and we — are to survive. Quite often people with little or no interest in "organized religion" take the lead when it comes to ecological issues and the need to save our natural environment.

Saint Francis of Assisi would be on the side of those who work to use our natural resources responsibly. Where are we? Do we leave it to those who have little interest in "organized religion"? Maybe this contributes to their lack of interest? A mature faith reveals the Creator at work in our forests, grasslands, rivers and lakes. Saint Paul said that we see God in his creation.

Still, it's also true that we can't stop with creation. We need to see through creation to the Creator who is our only source of true joy. To limit our vision to the forests, grasslands, lakes and rivers — to not embrace the Creator of all these things as our Father, too — is to leave ourselves open to ultimate frustration and disappointment. For God alone can satisfy the human heart. God alone. But never apart from the mountains, forests, grasslands, lakes, valleys, rivers and oceans.

Loving God, thank you for the gift of your creation;
help me to do my part to care for our natural environment
and to see you in all you have made. Amen.

Friday, Fifth Week of Lent

The first unit of society is the family. The family should look after its own and, in addition, as the early fathers said,

"Every home should have a Christ room in it, so that hospitality may be practiced." "The coat that hangs in your closet belongs to the poor." "If your brother is hungry it is your responsibility."

— DOROTHY DAY, *Meditations*

THE FAMILY in its various forms — two-parent families, single-parent families, young couples without children, older couples whose children are grown and gone, "blended" families, single and widowed people in the context of their extended family network — is the church's most basic unit, as well as the most basic unit of society. This truth carries many implications.

The home is where our most basic religious experiences happen. Home is where the heart is, and home is where our loving God is. When we leave home to attend Mass in our parish church we may feel that we leave the secular and the profane to go to the holy and the sacred. But the contrary is true. To leave home for church is simply to move from one form of God's presence to another. We find God in our family relationships and everyday tasks and we find God in church.

In our family we carry out the traditional works of mercy: we clothe the naked, feed the hungry, instruct the ignorant, give drink to the thirsty, care for the sick, and so forth. But it is also important for families of all kinds to reach out in some way appropriate for each family, to reach out to those with special needs. When we do this our family benefits far more than those we serve.

Loving God, thank you for being the very fabric
of my family relationships;
help me to be more sensitive to your presence there. Amen.

> *... though prayer for self is the first and plainest of Christian duties, the Apostles especially insist on another kind of prayer; prayer for others, for ourselves with others, for the Church, and for the world... Intercession is the characteristic of Christian worship, the privilege of the heavenly adoption, the exercise of the perfect and spiritual mind.*
>
> — JOHN HENRY NEWMAN, *Parochial and Plain Sermons*

IT IS EASY to forget the value and importance of simple prayer. How often do we pray for ourselves? Yes, we may beg God for help with this problem or that challenge we face. We may ask for God's help with all kinds of things. But how often do I simply pray for myself? How often do I simply abandon myself to God's will saying, "Do with me as you will, O God," or "Let your Spirit be in my heart and in my mind to guide me in all that I do"? This, Newman says, is the most obvious of Christian duties.

But prayer for others is also basic. Prayer for those we love, prayer for those we work with, prayer for the tired old world struggling to be free, prayer for our children, prayer for church and civic leaders. There are so many to pray for, and prayer is something we can do. We may not feel well informed about political issues, but we can pray. We may not be experts on theological debates in the church, but we can pray. We may not have a good grasp on the social problems of our day, but we can pray.

People are sick and suffering. We can pray for them. People slog through thick and thin, trying to make ends meet. We can pray for them. Young people face tremendous challenges and risks merely in growing up. We can pray for them. Our family lives from one week to the next, perhaps, or maybe from one crisis to the next. We can pray for ourselves, for our family, for all our needs. But how often do we do this?

Thank you, loving Father, for the gift of prayer;
help me to use it more than I do
for all the good purposes of prayer. Amen.

Passion (Palm) Sunday

We cannot know whether or not we love God, although there are strong indications for recognizing that we do love Him; but we can know whether we love our neighbor. And be certain that the more advanced you see you are in love for your neighbor the more advanced you will be in the love of God, for the love [God] has for us is so great that to repay us for our love of neighbor He will in a thousand ways increase the love we have for Him.

— SAINT TERESA OF AVILA, *The Interior Castle*

IT'S EASY to be pious, easy to lip-synch the liturgy, easy to do all the right religious things. It's easy to say you love God. It's not so easy to be genuinely Christian because this means that love of God and love of neighbor can never be separated.

You say you love God, but you have your doubts about your fellow human beings? You say you love God but other people give you a pain? You are not so unusual. In fact, you are like most who claim to be Christians.

It's true. We say we love God. We *want* to love God. But genuine love for other people is a trial. Other people are so, well . . . *difficult* to love. Other people irritate us. Other people get on our nerves. It's the same old song, the same old tune. But the message of the gospel rings as clear as a bell. " . . . those who do not love a brother or sister whom they have seen, cannot love God whom they have not seen" (1 Jn 4:20).

If anything, love for one another takes precedence over love for God, but the precedence is only apparent. For to love another person is to love God. If active care for another person means you must leave your prayers then the other person's needs take precedence over prayer.

Loving Father, thank you for the gift of other people to love; help me to love others with the love I have for you. Amen.

Monday of Holy Week

. . . there is a God who is alive . . . and His eye is also upon us; *and I am sure that He plans our life and that we do not quite belong to ourselves as it were. This God is no other than Christ, who we read about in our Bible and whose word and history is also deep in our hearts.*

— Vincent van Gogh,
The Complete Letters of Vincent van Gogh

Here we sit, on the cusp of the holiest week of the year; the holiest week of the year, but still the most basic question faces us: do we or do we not believe? Is our God alive, or is our God a mere idea, or principle, or theory? If we believe God to be alive it can only be because we *know* God to be alive through our own experience. We know through personal experience that we have an intimate, profoundly mysterious, deeply loving relationship with the Creator of the universe. This is faith. At rock bottom, this is faith, a relationship with all the ups and downs that characterize any relationship.

But there is a difference. A big difference. Because of this relationship we call faith, we do not exactly belong to ourselves any longer. We do not belong to ourselves. We belong to Christ who is deep in our hearts. This is a great mystery of the love that makes the universe spin through the vast reaches of space. This is a great mystery of the love that is at the center of our being.

God plans our life. In a sense, this is true. But in another sense it is not true. Two wills are at work here — God's will and our will, and God works with the choices we freely make, bringing everything to good in the end. Our task is to remain open to the influence of the Holy Spirit as we make our way through life and to know that God's love works with our choices whether they are the best possible choices or not. In all and above all there is mercy upon mercy.

Lord Jesus, thank you for being with me in all things;
help me to trust in your love and concern for me
and for all those I love. Amen.

Tuesday of Holy Week

A faith that just accepts is a child's faith and all right for children, but eventually you have to grow religiously as every other way, though some never do.

What people don't realize is how much religion costs. They think faith is a big electric blanket, when of course it is the cross. It is much harder to believe than not to believe....

Don't expect faith to clear things up for you. It is trust, not certainty...

— FLANNERY O'CONNOR, *The Habit of Being*

FAITH DOES NOT MEAN you shut down your brain, although it does mean that your brain has its limits. Faith does not mean that when it comes to religion intellectually you remain a child, although it does mean that you cultivate simplicity of heart like that found in children when they are at their best. We are supposed to become adults in every way, including our faith, our relationship with the Divine Mystery.

55

We become adults in all the ways we deal with the world and live our lives — our work, our grasp of economic realities, and so forth. Just so we are to gain an adult understanding of our faith. An adult Christian puts at least as much effort into understanding his or her faith as one puts into understanding professional or other work-related tasks.

Faith is a security blanket only as the cross is a security blanket. If faith isn't difficult sometimes it isn't truly faith. If what we want from faith is certainty, we are barking up the wrong tree. Often it is more difficult to believe than to not believe. On the other hand, flat-out skepticism can be the easiest thing in the world, and since when has the easy way been the best way to go?

Lord God, thank you for the gift of faith;
help me to live my faith on an adult level
and not to seek escape
when it turns out to be the cross. Amen.

Wednesday of Holy Week

How much you have loved us, Good Father, who "did not spare your only Son, but delivered Him up for us" (Rom 8:32), the ungodly! How you have loved us, for whom "He who thought it not robbery to be equal with you was made subject even to the death of the cross" (Phil 2:6–8).

— SAINT AUGUSTINE OF HIPPO, *Confessions*

SOMETIMES WE FIND IT difficult to believe in God's unconditional love for us. Sometimes we find it difficult to believe that God is like a passionate lover, pursuing us constantly, constantly longing for our love, constantly waiting for our return. We think of ourselves as seeking God, but God is seeking us.

We think of ourselves as begging God to be with us, but God begs us to be with Him.

Our God is a confluence of contradictions. We pray to God as our loving Father, which is true. But just about then God wants to love us as our loving Mother, to give birth to us in ways we did not expect. Jesus teaches us to call God our Father, then speaks of wanting to gather his people in a motherly way, "as a hen gathers her brood under her wings..." (Lk 13:34).

God is with us, loving us with a love that is infinite and unconditional. Not only this, but God lives in you, in each of us, at all times. What is there to fear if God lives in you? Feeling unloved or lonely all we need do is recall that God is closer to us than any human person ever could be. Sometimes we need to *feel* loved, of course, and at times like that we can ask God to help us feel loved. We are fragile human beings who need to feel, not just know.

God's love for us is so reliable that He gives us Himself. Freely, without price, God dwells in you. Be quiet, sit still, and be aware of this. Let it sink in. Deep.

Loving God, your love surrounds me and fills me
at all times and in all places;
help me to feel your love more deeply. Amen.

Holy Thursday

St. Bonaventure said that after the long fast of our Lord in the desert, when the angels came to minister to Him, they went first to the Blessed Mother to see what she had on her stove, and got the soup she had prepared and transported it to our Lord, who relished it the more because His Mother had prepared it. Of course.

— Dorothy Day, *Meditations*

HOLY THURSDAY HAS WONDERS. Holy Thursday has wonders and marvels to show us. If we quiet down and pay attention, if we quiet down and pay attention, Holy Thursday will hum a quiet song in our heart. Holy Thursday will hum a quiet song in our heart about the Bread of Life and the Lord Jesus who *is* the Bread of Life. Marvels and wonders.

Many people today puzzle over the meaning of the Eucharist. Some have "problems" with the teaching that the bread and wine become the Body and Blood of Jesus. Oh, imponderable. Can we believe this? Or does the bread and wine simply *represent* the Body and Blood of Jesus? Some say this must be it. It must. But what we have here is a failure to communicate.

Of course the bread and wine become the Body and Blood of Jesus. But what does this mean? For the Jewish Jesus "body and blood" was a phrase that meant, simply, "the whole person." So the bread and wine become the "whole person" of Jesus. It's as simple as that. No need to get excited. Be awestruck, instead. For the bread and wine become not just the "whole person" of Jesus, but *the whole person of the risen Christ* who is already present in our midst to begin with.

What does it mean — oh, mystery; oh, wonder — for bread and wine to become the whole person of the risen Christ? What do "resurrection" and "risen" mean? They speak marvels and wonders we experience but cannot grasp, that we know with the heart, not with the mind. Oh, marvels. Oh, wonders.

Loving God, thank you for the gift of the Eucharist;
help me to have a deeper respect and affection
for the grace it brings into my life. Amen.

This, then, is the effect of suffering, that it arrests us: that it puts, as it were, a finger upon us to ascertain for us our own individuality. But it does no more than this; if such a warning does not lead us through the stirrings of our conscience heavenwards, it does but imprison us in ourselves and make us selfish.

— John Henry Newman, *Parochial and Plain Sermons*

PERHAPS NO ONE can speak about the meaning of suffering except those who suffer or have suffered. But — to one degree or another — that includes all of us. No one gets out of this life without suffering. Even innocent children suffer. Some people say they cannot believe in God because innocent children suffer. This, of course, says something about the God they do not believe in, and perhaps they have an image of God not worth believing in. Perhaps the problem of suffering, more than anything else, leads us to clarify for ourselves what we mean when we say, "God."

Perhaps God "feels," as it were, much as we do about suffering. Or . . . perhaps suffering is where we most clearly encounter our own limitations and the mystery of existence. God says to Job: Where were you when I created the world? Here, smarty-pants, put up or shut up.

In the darkness of suffering, faith alone can make a difference, and at such times faith becomes a sheer act of the will, a naked act of trust with nothing apparent to justify it. Dying on the cross Jesus had no reason to abandon himself to his Father's love.

Suffering either pushes us to abandon ourselves to God in trust or it turns us in on ourselves in selfishness and self-pity. The choice is ours to make. We do make it, each and every one of us.

Loving God, when my life is marked by suffering
help me in the midst of the darkness to give myself
completely to you in trust and love. Amen.

Holy Saturday

It is good to love many things, for therein lies true strength;
whosoever loves much, performs and can accomplish much,
and what is done in love is well done.

— VINCENT VAN GOGH,
The Complete Letters of Vincent van Gogh

TODAY IS, perhaps, the ultimate in-between day. Neither here nor there. Yesterday was the day of the cross and death, tomorrow the day of Resurrection. But today...what shall we do with today? We wait. We wait, breathe evenly, watch as an early spring breeze touches the new green buds on the branches of a tree. If we are lucky there is sunshine today in the early spring, and we wait...we wait...

We might say that our entire life is one long Holy Saturday, neither here nor there. Life is an in-between experience. We come from mystery and we go into mystery, and we are in-between and on the way. But Holy Saturday — and a Holy Saturday life — is a time when the most appropriate virtue is hope. We hope, and our hope is not without reason. For unlike the first Holy Saturday, in our Holy Saturday we already know the power and light of the Resurrection.

We wait in the shadow of Good Friday, but the dawn of Easter is already on the horizon. So we sit. We wait quietly. Holy Saturday is a quiet day, a day to be alone perhaps, or a day to share a quiet, simple meal with family and friends, a day to quietly dust and clean, a day to quietly prepare for an Easter breakfast or dinner.

On Holy Saturday we unpack the quiet joy of being in-between this and that, here and there, and on the way. On Holy Saturday, if there is some sunshine and a few green buds, we calmly prepare ourselves . . . for what? For ecstasy.

Loving Father, thank you for the gift of Holy Saturday,
the day that is in-between; help me to live this day
in quiet hope of the Resurrection. Amen.

Easter Sunday

I don't really think the standard of judgment, the missing link . . . in my stories emerges from any religion but Christianity, because it concerns specifically Christ and the Incarnation, the fact that there has been a unique intervention in history. . . . As the Misfit said [in her short story, "The Misfit"], "He thrown everything off balance and it's nothing for you to do but follow Him or find some meanness."
— FLANNERY O'CONNOR, *The Habit of Being*

HERE THIS MORNING, early, a silent explosion with a blinding light. Perhaps. Or maybe a deafening silence and the stone rolls back from the entrance to the tomb, the sandy soil crunching quietly under the weight of the stone. Within, nothing. Within, nobody. Empty. Only the shroud the women wrapped him in is left. Empty, but the air crackles with a kind of electricity. Perhaps. Something happened here. Something happened. We will always know what, and we will never know precisely what. Something.

Resurrection. No room to be simple-minded. Not talking about a resuscitated corpse here. Talking about Resurrection, a word we use to talk about Something. A word we use to talk about Something the human mind cannot begin to understand. Something that happened. Something. Resurrection. It happened to Jesus after he died. Dead as can be, and it happened to him. Dead as can be, and it happens — is happening, will happen, has happened — to us, as well. To us.

Resurrection happened to Jesus, whatever it is. A new and completely better life. Resurrection is not merely a 2,000-year-old happening, however. It happens now. We know the Resurrection because it happens — is beginning to happen — to us. Right here, right now. It happens to us.

Jesus is risen. Alleluia. We are being raised, and we are on our way to Resurrection. Alleluia. Dead as can be, and it happens. To us. Alleluia.

Risen Savior, draw me to yourself
that I may share more fully
in the grace and joy of your Resurrection. Amen.

Spiritual Classics
Quoted in This Book

Augustine of Hippo: Selected Writings, translation and Introduction by Mary T. Clark. Paulist Press, 1984.

Meditations, by Dorothy Day. Newman Press, 1977.

John Henry Newman: Selected Sermons, edited with an Introduction by Ian Kerr. Paulist Press, 1994.

Teresa of Avila: The Interior Castle, translation by Kieran Kavanaugh, O.C.D. and Otilio Rodriguez, O.C.D. Paulist Press, 1979.

Van Gogh and God: A Creative Spiritual Quest, by Cliff Edwards. Loyola Press, 1989.

The Habit of Being: Letters of Flannery O'Connor, selected and edited by Sally Fitzgerald. Farrar, Straus & Giroux, 1979.

Published by Resurrection Press

Resurrection Press books and cassettes are available in your local religious bookstore. If you want to be on our mailing list for our up-to-date announcements, please write or phone:

Resurrection Press
P.O. Box 248, Williston Park, NY 11596
1-800-89 BOOKS